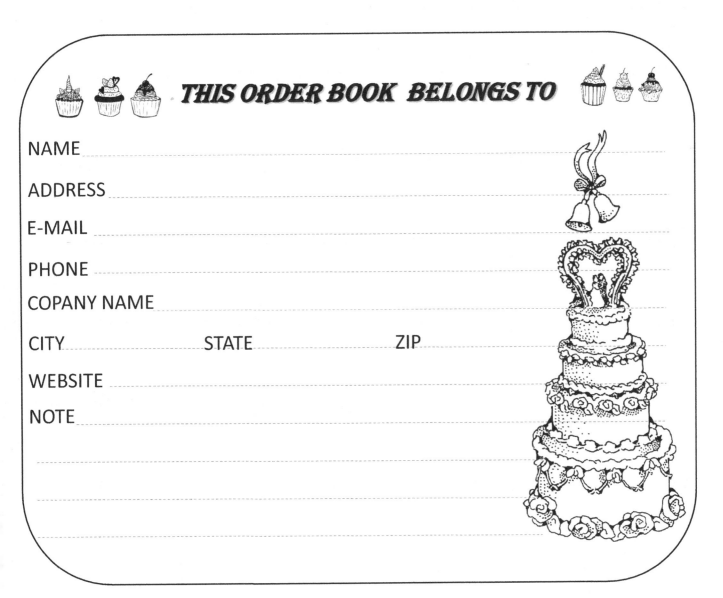

THIS ORDER BOOK BELONGS TO

NAME

ADDRESS

E-MAIL

PHONE

COPANY NAME

CITY   STATE   ZIP

WEBSITE

NOTE

Order Index

ORDER N	Order	Date	ORDER N	Order	Date
1			24		
2			25		
3			26		
4			27		
5			28		
6			29		
7			30		
8			31		
9			32		
10			33		
11			34		
12			35		
13			36		
14			37		
15			38		
16			39		
17			40		
18			41		
19			42		
20			43		
21			44		
22			45		
23			46		

Order Index

ORDER N	Order	Date	ORDER N	Order	Date
47			70		
48			71		
49			72		
50			73		
51			74		
52			75		
53			76		
54			77		
55			78		
56			79		
57			80		
58			81		
59			82		
60			83		
61			84		
62			85		
63			86		
64			87		
65			88		
66			89		
67			90		
68			91		
69			92		

Order Index

ORDER N	Order	Date	ORDER N	Order	Date
93			116		
94			117		
95			118		
96			119		
97			120		
98			121		
99			122		
100			123		
101			124		
102			125		
103			126		
104			127		
105			128		
106			129		
107			130		
108			131		
109			132		
110			133		
111			134		
112			135		
113			136		
114			137		
115			138		

Order date:	Pickup ☐	**CAKE**
Delivery date:	Delivery ☐	**ORDER**
Order N:		**FORM**

CUSTOMER DETAILS

Name:

Address:

E-mail: Phone:

CAKE DETAILS

Cake type:	Tier:
Quantify:	Cake size:
Flavor:	Shape:
Color scheme:	Frosting:
Filling:	Writing:

SPECIAL INSTRUCTIONS

PAYMENTS DETAILS

Total:	Deposit:	Total:
Cost:	Paid:	Paid:
Form of payment:		

Order date:	Pickup ☐	# CAKE
Delivery date:	Delivery ☐	# ORDER
Order N:		# FORM

CUSTOMER DETAILS

Name:

Address:

E-mail: Phone:

CAKE DETAILS

Cake type: Tier:

Quantify: Cake size:

Flavor: Shape:

Color scheme: Frosting:

Filling: Writing:

SPECIAL INSTRUCTIONS

PAYMENTS DETAILS

Total: Deposit: Total:

Cost: Paid: Paid:

Form of payment:

Order date: .... Pickup ☐

Delivery date: .... Delivery ☐

Order N: ....

CAKE ORDER FORM

CUSTOMER DETAILS

Name: ....

Address: ....

E-mail: .... Phone: ....

CAKE DETAILS

Cake type: .... Tier: ....

Quantify: .... Cake size: ....

Flavor: .... Shape: ....

Color scheme: .... Frosting: ....

Filling: .... Writing: ....

SPECIAL INSTRUCTIONS

....

....

....

....

....

PAYMENTS DETAILS

Total: .... Deposit: .... Total: ....

Cost: .... Paid: .... Paid: ....

Form of payment: ....

Order date: .... Pickup ☐

Delivery date: .... Delivery ☐

Order N: ....

CAKE ORDER FORM

CUSTOMER DETAILS

Name: ....

Address: ....

E-mail: .... Phone: ....

CAKE DETAILS

Cake type:	Tier: ....
Quantify:	Cake size: ....
Flavor:	Shape: ....
Color scheme:	Frosting: ....
Filling:	Writing: ....

SPECIAL INSTRUCTIONS

....

....

....

....

PAYMENTS DETAILS

Total:	Deposit:	Total: ....
Cost:	Paid:	Paid: ....
Form of payment:		

Order date:	Pickup ☐	**CAKE**
Delivery date:	Delivery ☐	**ORDER**
Order N:		**FORM**

CUSTOMER DETAILS

Name:

Address:

E-mail: Phone:

CAKE DETAILS

Cake type: Tier:

Quantify: Cake size:

Flavor: Shape:

Color scheme: Frosting:

Filling: Writing:

SPECIAL INSTRUCTIONS

PAYMENTS DETAILS

Total: Deposit: Total:

Cost: Paid: Paid:

Form of payment:

Order date: .... Pickup ☐ Delivery date: .... Delivery ☐ Order N:	**CAKE ORDER FORM**

CUSTOMER DETAILS

Name: ....

Address: ....

E-mail: .... Phone: ....

CAKE DETAILS

Cake type:	Tier: ....
Quantify:	Cake size: ....
Flavor:	Shape: ....
Color scheme:	Frosting: ....
Filling:	Writing: ....

SPECIAL INSTRUCTIONS

....

....

....

....

....

PAYMENTS DETAILS

Total: .... Deposit: .... Total: ....

Cost: .... Paid: .... Paid: ....

Form of payment: ....

Order date: .... Pickup ☐

Delivery date: .... Delivery ☐

Order N: ....

CAKE ORDER FORM

CUSTOMER DETAILS

Name:

Address:

E-mail: Phone:

CAKE DETAILS

Cake type: Tier:

Quantify: Cake size:

Flavor: Shape:

Color scheme: Frosting:

Filling: Writing:

SPECIAL INSTRUCTIONS

PAYMENTS DETAILS

Total: Deposit: Total:

Cost: Paid: Paid:

Form of payment:

Order date: .... Pickup ☐

Delivery date: .... Delivery ☐

Order N: ....

CAKE ORDER FORM

CUSTOMER DETAILS

Name: ....

Address: ....

E-mail: .... Phone: ....

CAKE DETAILS

Cake type: .... Tier: ....

Quantify: .... Cake size: ....

Flavor: .... Shape: ....

Color scheme: .... Frosting: ....

Filling: .... Writing: ....

SPECIAL INSTRUCTIONS

....

....

....

....

PAYMENTS DETAILS

Total: .... Deposit: .... Total: ....

Cost: .... Paid: .... Paid: ....

Form of payment: ....

Order date: .... Pickup ☐

Delivery date: .... Delivery ☐

Order N: ....

CAKE ORDER FORM

CUSTOMER DETAILS

Name: ....

Address: ....

E-mail: .... Phone: ....

CAKE DETAILS

Cake type: .... Tier: ....

Quantify: .... Cake size: ....

Flavor: .... Shape: ....

Color scheme: .... Frosting: ....

Filling: .... Writing: ....

SPECIAL INSTRUCTIONS

....

....

....

....

PAYMENTS DETAILS

Total: .... Deposit: .... Total: ....

Cost: .... Paid: .... Paid: ....

Form of payment: ....

Order date: .... Pickup ☐

Delivery date: .... Delivery ☐

Order N: ....

CAKE ORDER FORM

CUSTOMER DETAILS

Name: ....

Address: ....

E-mail: .... Phone: ....

CAKE DETAILS

Cake type: .... Tier: ....

Quantify: .... Cake size: ....

Flavor: .... Shape: ....

Color scheme: .... Frosting: ....

Filling: .... Writing: ....

SPECIAL INSTRUCTIONS

PAYMENTS DETAILS

Total: .... Deposit: .... Total: ....

Cost: .... Paid: .... Paid: ....

Form of payment: ....

Order date: .... Pickup ☐

Delivery date: .... Delivery ☐

Order N: ....

CAKE ORDER FORM

CUSTOMER DETAILS

Name:

Address:

E-mail: Phone:

CAKE DETAILS

Cake type: Tier:

Quantify: Cake size:

Flavor: Shape:

Color scheme: Frosting:

Filling: Writing:

SPECIAL INSTRUCTIONS

PAYMENTS DETAILS

Total: Deposit: Total:

Cost: Paid: Paid:

Form of payment:

		CAKE
Order date:	Pickup ☐	ORDER
Delivery date:	Delivery ☐	FORM
Order N:		

CUSTOMER DETAILS

Name:

Address:

E-mail: Phone:

CAKE DETAILS

Cake type: Tier:

Quantify: Cake size:

Flavor: Shape:

Color scheme: Frosting:

Filling: Writing:

SPECIAL INSTRUCTIONS

PAYMENTS DETAILS

Total: Deposit: Total:

Cost: Paid: Paid:

Form of payment:

Order date:	Pickup ☐	# CAKE ORDER FORM
Delivery date:	Delivery ☐	
Order N:		

CUSTOMER DETAILS

Name:

Address:

E-mail: Phone:

CAKE DETAILS

Cake type:	Tier:
Quantify:	Cake size:
Flavor:	Shape:
Color scheme:	Frosting:
Filling:	Writing:

SPECIAL INSTRUCTIONS

PAYMENTS DETAILS

Total:	Deposit:	Total:
Cost:	Paid:	Paid:
Form of payment:		

Order date: .... Pickup ☐

Delivery date: .... Delivery ☐

Order N: ....

CAKE ORDER FORM

CUSTOMER DETAILS

Name:

Address:

E-mail: Phone:

CAKE DETAILS

Cake type: Tier:

Quantify: Cake size:

Flavor: Shape:

Color scheme: Frosting:

Filling: Writing:

SPECIAL INSTRUCTIONS

PAYMENTS DETAILS

Total: Deposit: Total:

Cost: Paid: Paid:

Form of payment:

Order date:	Pickup ☐	### CAKE ORDER FORM
Delivery date:	Delivery ☐	
Order N:		

CUSTOMER DETAILS

Name:

Address:

E-mail: Phone:

CAKE DETAILS

Cake type: Tier:

Quantify: Cake size:

Flavor: Shape:

Color scheme: Frosting:

Filling: Writing:

SPECIAL INSTRUCTIONS

PAYMENTS DETAILS

Total: Deposit: Total:

Cost: Paid: Paid:

Form of payment:

Order date: .... Pickup ☐

Delivery date: .... Delivery ☐

Order N: ....

CAKE ORDER FORM

CUSTOMER DETAILS

Name:

Address:

E-mail: Phone:

CAKE DETAILS

Cake type:	Tier:
Quantify:	Cake size:
Flavor:	Shape:
Color scheme:	Frosting:
Filling:	Writing:

SPECIAL INSTRUCTIONS

PAYMENTS DETAILS

Total:	Deposit:	Total:
Cost:	Paid:	Paid:
Form of payment:		

Order date: .... Pickup ☐

Delivery date: .... Delivery ☐

Order N: ....

CAKE ORDER FORM

CUSTOMER DETAILS

Name:

Address:

E-mail: Phone:

CAKE DETAILS

Cake type: Tier:

Quantify: Cake size:

Flavor: Shape:

Color scheme: Frosting:

Filling: Writing:

SPECIAL INSTRUCTIONS

PAYMENTS DETAILS

Total: Deposit: Total:

Cost: Paid: Paid:

Form of payment:

Order date: .... Pickup ☐

Delivery date: .... Delivery ☐

Order N: ....

CAKE ORDER FORM

CUSTOMER DETAILS

Name: ....

Address: ....

E-mail: .... Phone: ....

CAKE DETAILS

Cake type: .... Tier: ....

Quantify: .... Cake size: ....

Flavor: .... Shape: ....

Color scheme: .... Frosting: ....

Filling: .... Writing: ....

SPECIAL INSTRUCTIONS

....

....

....

....

....

PAYMENTS DETAILS

Total: .... Deposit: .... Total: ....

Cost: .... Paid: .... Paid: ....

Form of payment: ....

Order date: .... Pickup ☐

Delivery date: .... Delivery ☐

Order N: ....

CAKE ORDER FORM

CUSTOMER DETAILS

Name:

Address:

E-mail: Phone:

CAKE DETAILS

Cake type:	Tier:
Quantify:	Cake size:
Flavor:	Shape:
Color scheme:	Frosting:
Filling:	Writing:

SPECIAL INSTRUCTIONS

PAYMENTS DETAILS

Total:	Deposit:	Total:
Cost:	Paid:	Paid:
Form of payment:		

Order date: .... Pickup ☐

Delivery date: .... Delivery ☐

Order N: ....

CAKE ORDER FORM

CUSTOMER DETAILS

Name: ....

Address: ....

E-mail: .... Phone: ....

CAKE DETAILS

Cake type: .... Tier: ....

Quantify: .... Cake size: ....

Flavor: .... Shape: ....

Color scheme: .... Frosting: ....

Filling: .... Writing: ....

SPECIAL INSTRUCTIONS

....

....

....

....

PAYMENTS DETAILS

Total: .... Deposit: .... Total: ....

Cost: .... Paid: .... Paid: ....

Form of payment: ....

Order date: _____ Pickup ☐

Delivery date: _____ Delivery ☐

Order N: _____

CAKE ORDER FORM

CUSTOMER DETAILS

Name:

Address:

E-mail: Phone:

CAKE DETAILS

Cake type: Tier:

Quantify: Cake size:

Flavor: Shape:

Color scheme: Frosting:

Filling: Writing:

SPECIAL INSTRUCTIONS

PAYMENTS DETAILS

Total: Deposit: Total:

Cost: Paid: Paid:

Form of payment:

Order date: .... Pickup ☐

Delivery date: .... Delivery ☐

Order N: ....

CAKE ORDER FORM

CUSTOMER DETAILS

Name: ....

Address: ....

E-mail: .... Phone: ....

CAKE DETAILS

Cake type: .... Tier: ....

Quantify: .... Cake size: ....

Flavor: .... Shape: ....

Color scheme: .... Frosting: ....

Filling: .... Writing: ....

SPECIAL INSTRUCTIONS

....

....

....

....

PAYMENTS DETAILS

Total: .... Deposit: .... Total: ....

Cost: .... Paid: .... Paid: ....

Form of payment: ....

Order date:	Pickup ☐
Delivery date:	Delivery ☐
Order N:	

CAKE ORDER FORM

CUSTOMER DETAILS

Name:

Address:

E-mail: Phone:

CAKE DETAILS

Cake type: Tier:

Quantify: Cake size:

Flavor: Shape:

Color scheme: Frosting:

Filling: Writing:

SPECIAL INSTRUCTIONS

PAYMENTS DETAILS

Total: Deposit: Total:

Cost: Paid: Paid:

Form of payment:

Order date: .... Pickup ☐

Delivery date: .... Delivery ☐

Order N: ....

CAKE ORDER FORM

CUSTOMER DETAILS

Name: ....

Address: ....

E-mail: .... Phone: ....

CAKE DETAILS

Cake type: .... Tier: ....

Quantify: .... Cake size: ....

Flavor: .... Shape: ....

Color scheme: .... Frosting: ....

Filling: .... Writing: ....

SPECIAL INSTRUCTIONS

....

....

....

....

PAYMENTS DETAILS

Total: .... Deposit: .... Total: ....

Cost: .... Paid: .... Paid: ....

Form of payment: ....

Order date:	Pickup ☐	**CAKE**
Delivery date:	Delivery ☐	**ORDER**
Order N:		**FORM**

CUSTOMER DETAILS

Name: ....

Address: ....

E-mail: .... Phone: ....

CAKE DETAILS

Cake type: .... Tier: ....

Quantify: .... Cake size: ....

Flavor: .... Shape: ....

Color scheme: .... Frosting: ....

Filling: .... Writing: ....

SPECIAL INSTRUCTIONS

....

....

....

....

PAYMENTS DETAILS

Total: .... Deposit: .... Total: ....

Cost: .... Paid: .... Paid: ....

Form of payment: ....

	Pickup ☐	**CAKE**
Order date:	Delivery ☐	**ORDER**
Delivery date:		**FORM**
Order N:		

CUSTOMER DETAILS

Name:

Address:

E-mail: Phone:

CAKE DETAILS

Cake type:	Tier:
Quantify:	Cake size:
Flavor:	Shape:
Color scheme:	Frosting:
Filling:	Writing:

SPECIAL INSTRUCTIONS

PAYMENTS DETAILS

Total:	Deposit:	Total:
Cost:	Paid:	Paid:
Form of payment:		

CAKE ORDER FORM

Order date: .... Pickup ☐
Delivery date: .... Delivery ☐
Order N: ....

CUSTOMER DETAILS

Name:
Address:
E-mail: Phone:

CAKE DETAILS

Cake type: Tier:
Quantify: Cake size:
Flavor: Shape:
Color scheme: Frosting:
Filling: Writing:

SPECIAL INSTRUCTIONS

PAYMENTS DETAILS

Total: Deposit: Total:
Cost: Paid: Paid:
Form of payment:

Order date:	Pickup ☐
Delivery date:	Delivery ☐
Order N:	

CAKE ORDER FORM

CUSTOMER DETAILS

Name:

Address:

E-mail: Phone:

CAKE DETAILS

Cake type:	Tier:
Quantify:	Cake size:
Flavor:	Shape:
Color scheme:	Frosting:
Filling:	Writing:

SPECIAL INSTRUCTIONS

PAYMENTS DETAILS

Total:	Deposit:	Total:
Cost:	Paid:	Paid:
Form of payment:		

Order date:	Pickup ☐
Delivery date:	Delivery ☐
Order N:	

CAKE ORDER FORM

CUSTOMER DETAILS

Name:

Address:

E-mail: Phone:

CAKE DETAILS

Cake type: Tier:

Quantify: Cake size:

Flavor: Shape:

Color scheme: Frosting:

Filling: Writing:

SPECIAL INSTRUCTIONS

PAYMENTS DETAILS

Total: Deposit: Total:

Cost: Paid: Paid:

Form of payment:

Order date: _____ Pickup ☐

Delivery date: _____ Delivery ☐

Order N: _____

CAKE ORDER FORM

CUSTOMER DETAILS

Name: _____

Address: _____

E-mail: _____ Phone: _____

CAKE DETAILS

Cake type: _____ Tier: _____

Quantify: _____ Cake size: _____

Flavor: _____ Shape: _____

Color scheme: _____ Frosting: _____

Filling: _____ Writing: _____

SPECIAL INSTRUCTIONS

_____

_____

_____

_____

PAYMENTS DETAILS

Total: _____ Deposit: _____ Total: _____

Cost: _____ Paid: _____ Paid: _____

Form of payment: _____

Order date: .... Pickup ☐

Delivery date: .... Delivery ☐

Order N: ....

CAKE ORDER FORM

CUSTOMER DETAILS

Name:

Address:

E-mail: Phone:

CAKE DETAILS

Cake type: Tier:

Quantify: Cake size:

Flavor: Shape:

Color scheme: Frosting:

Filling: Writing:

SPECIAL INSTRUCTIONS

PAYMENTS DETAILS

Total: Deposit: Total:

Cost: Paid: Paid:

Form of payment:

Order date: _____ Pickup ☐

Delivery date: _____ Delivery ☐

Order N: _____

CAKE ORDER FORM

CUSTOMER DETAILS

Name: _____

Address: _____

E-mail: _____ Phone: _____

CAKE DETAILS

Cake type: _____ Tier: _____

Quantify: _____ Cake size: _____

Flavor: _____ Shape: _____

Color scheme: _____ Frosting: _____

Filling: _____ Writing: _____

SPECIAL INSTRUCTIONS

_____

_____

_____

_____

PAYMENTS DETAILS

Total: _____ Deposit: _____ Total: _____

Cost: _____ Paid: _____ Paid: _____

Form of payment: _____

Order date:	Pickup ☐	# CAKE
Delivery date:	Delivery ☐	# ORDER
Order N:		# FORM

CUSTOMER DETAILS

Name:

Address:

E-mail: Phone:

CAKE DETAILS

Cake type: Tier:

Quantify: Cake size:

Flavor: Shape:

Color scheme: Frosting:

Filling: Writing:

SPECIAL INSTRUCTIONS

PAYMENTS DETAILS

Total:	Deposit:	Total:
Cost:	Paid:	Paid:
Form of payment:		

Order date: .... Pickup ☐

Delivery date: .... Delivery ☐

Order N: ....

CAKE ORDER FORM

CUSTOMER DETAILS

Name: ....

Address: ....

E-mail: ....　　　Phone: ....

CAKE DETAILS

Cake type: ....　　　Tier: ....

Quantify: ....　　　Cake size: ....

Flavor: ....　　　Shape: ....

Color scheme: ....　　　Frosting: ....

Filling: ....　　　Writing: ....

SPECIAL INSTRUCTIONS

PAYMENTS DETAILS

Total: ....　　Deposit: ....　　Total: ....

Cost: ....　　Paid: ....　　Paid: ....

Form of payment: ....

Order date:	Pickup ☐	# CAKE
Delivery date:	Delivery ☐	# ORDER
Order N:		# FORM

CUSTOMER DETAILS

Name:

Address:

E-mail: Phone:

CAKE DETAILS

Cake type: Tier:

Quantify: Cake size:

Flavor: Shape:

Color scheme: Frosting:

Filling: Writing:

SPECIAL INSTRUCTIONS

PAYMENTS DETAILS

Total: Deposit: Total:

Cost: Paid: Paid:

Form of payment:

Order date:	Pickup ☐
Delivery date:	Delivery ☐
Order N:	

CAKE ORDER FORM

CUSTOMER DETAILS

Name:

Address:

E-mail: Phone:

CAKE DETAILS

Cake type: Tier:

Quantify: Cake size:

Flavor: Shape:

Color scheme: Frosting:

Filling: Writing:

SPECIAL INSTRUCTIONS

PAYMENTS DETAILS

Total: Deposit: Total:

Cost: Paid: Paid:

Form of payment:

Order date: .... Pickup ☐

Delivery date: .... Delivery ☐

Order N: ....

CAKE ORDER FORM

CUSTOMER DETAILS

Name: ....

Address: ....

E-mail: .... Phone: ....

CAKE DETAILS

Cake type: .... Tier: ....

Quantify: .... Cake size: ....

Flavor: .... Shape: ....

Color scheme: .... Frosting: ....

Filling: .... Writing: ....

SPECIAL INSTRUCTIONS

PAYMENTS DETAILS

Total: .... Deposit: .... Total: ....

Cost: .... Paid: .... Paid: ....

Form of payment: ....

Order date:	Pickup ☐	**CAKE**
Delivery date:	Delivery ☐	**ORDER**
Order N:		**FORM**

CUSTOMER DETAILS

Name: ....

Address: ....

E-mail: .... Phone: ....

CAKE DETAILS

Cake type:	Tier: ....
Quantify:	Cake size: ....
Flavor:	Shape: ....
Color scheme:	Frosting: ....
Filling:	Writing: ....

SPECIAL INSTRUCTIONS

....

....

....

....

PAYMENTS DETAILS

Total:	Deposit:	Total: ....
Cost:	Paid:	Paid: ....
Form of payment:		

Order date: .... Pickup ☐

Delivery date: .... Delivery ☐

Order N: ....

CAKE ORDER FORM

CUSTOMER DETAILS

Name:

Address:

E-mail: Phone:

CAKE DETAILS

Cake type: Tier:

Quantify: Cake size:

Flavor: Shape:

Color scheme: Frosting:

Filling: Writing:

SPECIAL INSTRUCTIONS

PAYMENTS DETAILS

Total: Deposit: Total:

Cost: Paid: Paid:

Form of payment:

Order date: .... Pickup ☐

Delivery date: .... Delivery ☐

Order N: ....

CAKE ORDER FORM

CUSTOMER DETAILS

Name:

Address:

E-mail: Phone:

CAKE DETAILS

Cake type:	Tier:
Quantify:	Cake size:
Flavor:	Shape:
Color scheme:	Frosting:
Filling:	Writing:

SPECIAL INSTRUCTIONS

PAYMENTS DETAILS

Total:	Deposit:	Total:
Cost:	Paid:	Paid:
Form of payment:		

Order date:	Pickup ☐	**CAKE**
Delivery date:	Delivery ☐	**ORDER**
Order N:		**FORM**

CUSTOMER DETAILS

Name:

Address:

E-mail: Phone:

CAKE DETAILS

Cake type:	Tier:
Quantify:	Cake size:
Flavor:	Shape:
Color scheme:	Frosting:
Filling:	Writing:

SPECIAL INSTRUCTIONS

PAYMENTS DETAILS

Total:	Deposit:	Total:
Cost:	Paid:	Paid:
Form of payment:		

Order date: _____ Pickup ☐

Delivery date: _____ Delivery ☐

Order N: _____

CAKE ORDER FORM

CUSTOMER DETAILS

Name:

Address:

E-mail: Phone:

CAKE DETAILS

Cake type:	Tier:
Quantify:	Cake size:
Flavor:	Shape:
Color scheme:	Frosting:
Filling:	Writing:

SPECIAL INSTRUCTIONS

PAYMENTS DETAILS

Total:	Deposit:	Total:
Cost:	Paid:	Paid:
Form of payment:		

Order date: .... Pickup ☐

Delivery date: .... Delivery ☐

Order N: ....

CAKE ORDER FORM

CUSTOMER DETAILS

Name:

Address:

E-mail: Phone:

CAKE DETAILS

Cake type: Tier:

Quantify: Cake size:

Flavor: Shape:

Color scheme: Frosting:

Filling: Writing:

SPECIAL INSTRUCTIONS

PAYMENTS DETAILS

Total: Deposit: Total:

Cost: Paid: Paid:

Form of payment:

Order date: .... Pickup ☐

Delivery date: .... Delivery ☐

Order N: ....

CAKE ORDER FORM

CUSTOMER DETAILS

Name: ....

Address: ....

E-mail: .... Phone: ....

CAKE DETAILS

Cake type: .... Tier: ....

Quantify: .... Cake size: ....

Flavor: .... Shape: ....

Color scheme: .... Frosting: ....

Filling: .... Writing: ....

SPECIAL INSTRUCTIONS

....

....

....

....

PAYMENTS DETAILS

Total: .... Deposit: .... Total: ....

Cost: .... Paid: .... Paid: ....

Form of payment: ....

Order date:	Pickup ☐	**CAKE ORDER FORM**
Delivery date:	Delivery ☐	
Order N:		

CUSTOMER DETAILS

Name:

Address:

E-mail: Phone:

CAKE DETAILS

Cake type:	Tier:
Quantify:	Cake size:
Flavor:	Shape:
Color scheme:	Frosting:
Filling:	Writing:

SPECIAL INSTRUCTIONS

PAYMENTS DETAILS

Total:	Deposit:	Total:
Cost:	Paid:	Paid:
Form of payment:		

Order date: .... Pickup ☐

Delivery date: .... Delivery ☐

Order N: ....

CAKE ORDER FORM

CUSTOMER DETAILS

Name: ....

Address: ....

E-mail: .... Phone: ....

CAKE DETAILS

Cake type: .... Tier: ....

Quantify: .... Cake size: ....

Flavor: .... Shape: ....

Color scheme: .... Frosting: ....

Filling: .... Writing: ....

SPECIAL INSTRUCTIONS

....

....

....

....

PAYMENTS DETAILS

Total: .... Deposit: .... Total: ....

Cost: .... Paid: .... Paid: ....

Form of payment: ....

Order date: .... Pickup ☐

Delivery date: .... Delivery ☐

Order N: ....

CAKE ORDER FORM

CUSTOMER DETAILS

Name: ....

Address: ....

E-mail: .... Phone: ....

CAKE DETAILS

Cake type: .... Tier: ....

Quantify: .... Cake size: ....

Flavor: .... Shape: ....

Color scheme: .... Frosting: ....

Filling: .... Writing: ....

SPECIAL INSTRUCTIONS

....

....

....

....

PAYMENTS DETAILS

Total: .... Deposit: .... Total: ....

Cost: .... Paid: .... Paid: ....

Form of payment: ....

Order date: .... Pickup ☐

Delivery date: .... Delivery ☐

Order N: ....

CAKE ORDER FORM

CUSTOMER DETAILS

Name: ....

Address: ....

E-mail: .... Phone: ....

CAKE DETAILS

Cake type: .... Tier: ....

Quantify: .... Cake size: ....

Flavor: .... Shape: ....

Color scheme: .... Frosting: ....

Filling: .... Writing: ....

SPECIAL INSTRUCTIONS

....

....

....

....

PAYMENTS DETAILS

Total: .... Deposit: .... Total: ....

Cost: .... Paid: .... Paid: ....

Form of payment: ....

Order date:	Pickup ☐
Delivery date:	Delivery ☐
Order N:	

CAKE ORDER FORM

CUSTOMER DETAILS

Name:

Address:

E-mail: Phone:

CAKE DETAILS

Cake type: Tier:

Quantify: Cake size:

Flavor: Shape:

Color scheme: Frosting:

Filling: Writing:

SPECIAL INSTRUCTIONS

PAYMENTS DETAILS

Total: Deposit: Total:

Cost: Paid: Paid:

Form of payment:

Order date: .... Pickup ☐

Delivery date: .... Delivery ☐

Order N: ....

CAKE ORDER FORM

CUSTOMER DETAILS

Name: ....

Address: ....

E-mail: .... Phone: ....

CAKE DETAILS

Cake type: .... Tier: ....

Quantify: .... Cake size: ....

Flavor: .... Shape: ....

Color scheme: .... Frosting: ....

Filling: .... Writing: ....

SPECIAL INSTRUCTIONS

PAYMENTS DETAILS

Total: .... Deposit: .... Total: ....

Cost: .... Paid: .... Paid: ....

Form of payment: ....

Order date:	Pickup ☐		**CAKE**
Delivery date:	Delivery ☐		**ORDER**
Order N:			**FORM**

CUSTOMER DETAILS

Name:

Address:

E-mail: Phone:

CAKE DETAILS

Cake type:	Tier:
Quantify:	Cake size:
Flavor:	Shape:
Color scheme:	Frosting:
Filling:	Writing:

SPECIAL INSTRUCTIONS

PAYMENTS DETAILS

Total:	Deposit:	Total:
Cost:	Paid:	Paid:
Form of payment:		

Order date:	Pickup ☐	**CAKE ORDER FORM**
Delivery date:	Delivery ☐	
Order N:		

CUSTOMER DETAILS

Name:

Address:

E-mail: Phone:

CAKE DETAILS

Cake type:	Tier:
Quantify:	Cake size:
Flavor:	Shape:
Color scheme:	Frosting:
Filling:	Writing:

SPECIAL INSTRUCTIONS

PAYMENTS DETAILS

Total:	Deposit:	Total:
Cost:	Paid:	Paid:
Form of payment:		

	Order date:	Pickup ☐	# CAKE
	Delivery date:	Delivery ☐	# ORDER
	Order N:		# FORM

CUSTOMER DETAILS

Name:

Address:

E-mail: Phone:

CAKE DETAILS

Cake type:	Tier:
Quantify:	Cake size:
Flavor:	Shape:
Color scheme:	Frosting:
Filling:	Writing:

SPECIAL INSTRUCTIONS

PAYMENTS DETAILS

Total:	Deposit:	Total:
Cost:	Paid:	Paid:
Form of payment:		

Order date: .... Pickup ☐

Delivery date: .... Delivery ☐

Order N: ....

CAKE ORDER FORM

CUSTOMER DETAILS

Name:

Address:

E-mail: Phone:

CAKE DETAILS

Cake type: Tier:

Quantify: Cake size:

Flavor: Shape:

Color scheme: Frosting:

Filling: Writing:

SPECIAL INSTRUCTIONS

PAYMENTS DETAILS

Total: Deposit: Total:

Cost: Paid: Paid:

Form of payment:

Order date: .... Pickup ☐ Delivery date: .... Delivery ☐ Order N:	**CAKE ORDER FORM**

CUSTOMER DETAILS

Name:

Address:

E-mail: Phone:

CAKE DETAILS

Cake type: Tier:

Quantify: Cake size:

Flavor: Shape:

Color scheme: Frosting:

Filling: Writing:

SPECIAL INSTRUCTIONS

PAYMENTS DETAILS

Total: Deposit: Total:

Cost: Paid: Paid:

Form of payment:

Order date:	Pickup ☐	**CAKE**
Delivery date:	Delivery ☐	**ORDER**
Order N:		**FORM**

CUSTOMER DETAILS

Name:

Address:

E-mail: Phone:

CAKE DETAILS

Cake type:	Tier:
Quantify:	Cake size:
Flavor:	Shape:
Color scheme:	Frosting:
Filling:	Writing:

SPECIAL INSTRUCTIONS

PAYMENTS DETAILS

Total:	Deposit:	Total:
Cost:	Paid:	Paid:
Form of payment:		

Order date: .... Pickup ☐

Delivery date: .... Delivery ☐

Order N: ....

CAKE ORDER FORM

CUSTOMER DETAILS

Name:

Address:

E-mail: Phone:

CAKE DETAILS

Cake type:	Tier:
Quantify:	Cake size:
Flavor:	Shape:
Color scheme:	Frosting:
Filling:	Writing:

SPECIAL INSTRUCTIONS

PAYMENTS DETAILS

Total:	Deposit:	Total:
Cost:	Paid:	Paid:
Form of payment:		

Order date:	Pickup ☐	**CAKE ORDER FORM**
Delivery date:	Delivery ☐	
Order N:		

CUSTOMER DETAILS

Name:

Address:

E-mail: Phone:

CAKE DETAILS

Cake type:	Tier:
Quantify:	Cake size:
Flavor:	Shape:
Color scheme:	Frosting:
Filling:	Writing:

SPECIAL INSTRUCTIONS

PAYMENTS DETAILS

Total:	Deposit:	Total:
Cost:	Paid:	Paid:
Form of payment:		

Order date:	Pickup	☐	
Delivery date:	Delivery	☐	
Order N:			

CAKE ORDER FORM

CUSTOMER DETAILS

Name:

Address:

E-mail: Phone:

CAKE DETAILS

Cake type:	Tier:
Quantify:	Cake size:
Flavor:	Shape:
Color scheme:	Frosting:
Filling:	Writing:

SPECIAL INSTRUCTIONS

PAYMENTS DETAILS

Total:	Deposit:	Total:
Cost:	Paid:	Paid:
Form of payment:		

Order date:	Pickup ☐	**CAKE**
Delivery date:	Delivery ☐	**ORDER**
Order N:		**FORM**

CUSTOMER DETAILS

Name:

Address:

E-mail: Phone:

CAKE DETAILS

Cake type:	Tier:
Quantify:	Cake size:
Flavor:	Shape:
Color scheme:	Frosting:
Filling:	Writing:

SPECIAL INSTRUCTIONS

PAYMENTS DETAILS

Total:	Deposit:	Total:
Cost:	Paid:	Paid:
Form of payment:		

Order date: _____ Pickup ☐

Delivery date: _____ Delivery ☐

Order N: _____

CAKE ORDER FORM

CUSTOMER DETAILS

Name:

Address:

E-mail: Phone:

CAKE DETAILS

Cake type: Tier:

Quantify: Cake size:

Flavor: Shape:

Color scheme: Frosting:

Filling: Writing:

SPECIAL INSTRUCTIONS

PAYMENTS DETAILS

Total: Deposit: Total:

Cost: Paid: Paid:

Form of payment:

Order date: .... Pickup ☐

Delivery date: .... Delivery ☐

Order N: ....

CAKE ORDER FORM

CUSTOMER DETAILS

Name: ....

Address: ....

E-mail: .... Phone: ....

CAKE DETAILS

Cake type: .... Tier: ....

Quantify: .... Cake size: ....

Flavor: .... Shape: ....

Color scheme: .... Frosting: ....

Filling: .... Writing: ....

SPECIAL INSTRUCTIONS

....

....

....

....

....

PAYMENTS DETAILS

Total: .... Deposit: .... Total: ....

Cost: .... Paid: .... Paid: ....

Form of payment: ....

Order date: .... Pickup ☐

Delivery date: .... Delivery ☐

Order N: ....

CAKE ORDER FORM

CUSTOMER DETAILS

Name:

Address:

E-mail: Phone:

CAKE DETAILS

Cake type: Tier:

Quantify: Cake size:

Flavor: Shape:

Color scheme: Frosting:

Filling: Writing:

SPECIAL INSTRUCTIONS

PAYMENTS DETAILS

Total: Deposit: Total:

Cost: Paid: Paid:

Form of payment:

Order date: .... Pickup ☐

Delivery date: .... Delivery ☐

Order N: ....

CAKE ORDER FORM

CUSTOMER DETAILS

Name: ....

Address: ....

E-mail: .... Phone: ....

CAKE DETAILS

Cake type: .... Tier: ....

Quantify: .... Cake size: ....

Flavor: .... Shape: ....

Color scheme: .... Frosting: ....

Filling: .... Writing: ....

SPECIAL INSTRUCTIONS

....

....

....

....

PAYMENTS DETAILS

Total: .... Deposit: .... Total: ....

Cost: .... Paid: .... Paid: ....

Form of payment: ....

Order date: .... Pickup ☐

Delivery date: .... Delivery ☐

Order N: ....

CAKE ORDER FORM

CUSTOMER DETAILS

Name: ....

Address: ....

E-mail: .... Phone: ....

CAKE DETAILS

Cake type: .... Tier: ....

Quantify: .... Cake size: ....

Flavor: .... Shape: ....

Color scheme: .... Frosting: ....

Filling: .... Writing: ....

SPECIAL INSTRUCTIONS

....

....

....

....

PAYMENTS DETAILS

Total: .... Deposit: .... Total: ....

Cost: .... Paid: .... Paid: ....

Form of payment: ....

Order date:	Pickup ☐	**CAKE**
Delivery date:	Delivery ☐	**ORDER**
Order N:		**FORM**

CUSTOMER DETAILS

Name:

Address:

E-mail: Phone:

CAKE DETAILS

Cake type:	Tier:
Quantify:	Cake size:
Flavor:	Shape:
Color scheme:	Frosting:
Filling:	Writing:

SPECIAL INSTRUCTIONS

PAYMENTS DETAILS

Total:	Deposit:	Total:
Cost:	Paid:	Paid:
Form of payment:		

	Pickup ☐	# CAKE ORDER FORM

Order date: .... Pickup ☐

Delivery date: .... Delivery ☐

Order N: ....

CUSTOMER DETAILS

Name: ....

Address: ....

E-mail: .... Phone: ....

CAKE DETAILS

Cake type: .... Tier: ....

Quantify: .... Cake size: ....

Flavor: .... Shape: ....

Color scheme: .... Frosting: ....

Filling: .... Writing: ....

SPECIAL INSTRUCTIONS

....

....

....

....

PAYMENTS DETAILS

Total: .... Deposit: .... Total: ....

Cost: .... Paid: .... Paid: ....

Form of payment: ....

Order date:	....	Pickup	☐
Delivery date:	....	Delivery	☐
	Order N:	....	

CAKE ORDER FORM

CUSTOMER DETAILS

Name:

Address:

E-mail: | Phone:

CAKE DETAILS

Cake type:	Tier:
Quantify:	Cake size:
Flavor:	Shape:
Color scheme:	Frosting:
Filling:	Writing:

SPECIAL INSTRUCTIONS

PAYMENTS DETAILS

Total:	Deposit:	Total:
Cost:	Paid:	Paid:
Form of payment:		

	Order date:	Pickup ☐	**CAKE**
	Delivery date:	Delivery ☐	**ORDER**
	Order N:		**FORM**

CUSTOMER DETAILS

Name:

Address:

E-mail: Phone:

CAKE DETAILS

Cake type:	Tier:
Quantify:	Cake size:
Flavor:	Shape:
Color scheme:	Frosting:
Filling:	Writing:

SPECIAL INSTRUCTIONS

PAYMENTS DETAILS

Total:	Deposit:	Total:
Cost:	**Paid:**	Paid:
Form of payment:		

Order date: .... Pickup ☐

Delivery date: .... Delivery ☐

Order N: ....

CAKE ORDER FORM

CUSTOMER DETAILS

Name: ....

Address: ....

E-mail: .... Phone: ....

CAKE DETAILS

Cake type: .... Tier: ....

Quantify: .... Cake size: ....

Flavor: .... Shape: ....

Color scheme: .... Frosting: ....

Filling: .... Writing: ....

SPECIAL INSTRUCTIONS

PAYMENTS DETAILS

Total: .... Deposit: .... Total: ....

Cost: .... Paid: .... Paid: ....

Form of payment: ....

CAKE ORDER FORM

Order date: .... Pickup ☐

Delivery date: .... Delivery ☐

Order N: ....

CUSTOMER DETAILS

Name:

Address:

E-mail: Phone:

CAKE DETAILS

Cake type:	Tier:
Quantify:	Cake size:
Flavor:	Shape:
Color scheme:	Frosting:
Filling:	Writing:

SPECIAL INSTRUCTIONS

PAYMENTS DETAILS

Total:	Deposit:	Total:
Cost:	Paid:	Paid:
Form of payment:		

Order date:	Pickup ☐	**CAKE**
Delivery date:	Delivery ☐	**ORDER**
Order N:		**FORM**

CUSTOMER DETAILS

Name:

Address:

E-mail: Phone:

CAKE DETAILS

Cake type: Tier:

Quantify: Cake size:

Flavor: Shape:

Color scheme: Frosting:

Filling: Writing:

SPECIAL INSTRUCTIONS

PAYMENTS DETAILS

Total: Deposit: Total:

Cost: Paid: Paid:

Form of payment:

Order date: .... Pickup ☐

Delivery date: .... Delivery ☐

Order N: ....

CAKE ORDER FORM

CUSTOMER DETAILS

Name: ....

Address: ....

E-mail: .... Phone: ....

CAKE DETAILS

Cake type: .... Tier: ....

Quantify: .... Cake size: ....

Flavor: .... Shape: ....

Color scheme: .... Frosting: ....

Filling: .... Writing: ....

SPECIAL INSTRUCTIONS

....

....

....

....

PAYMENTS DETAILS

Total: .... Deposit: .... Total: ....

Cost: .... Paid: .... Paid: ....

Form of payment: ....

Order date: .... Pickup ☐

Delivery date: .... Delivery ☐

Order N: ....

CAKE ORDER FORM

CUSTOMER DETAILS

Name:

Address:

E-mail: Phone:

CAKE DETAILS

Cake type: Tier:

Quantify: Cake size:

Flavor: Shape:

Color scheme: Frosting:

Filling: Writing:

SPECIAL INSTRUCTIONS

PAYMENTS DETAILS

Total: Deposit: Total:

Cost: Paid: Paid:

Form of payment:

Order date:	Pickup ☐	**CAKE**
Delivery date:	Delivery ☐	**ORDER**
Order N:		**FORM**

CUSTOMER DETAILS

Name:

Address:

E-mail: Phone:

CAKE DETAILS

Cake type: Tier:

Quantify: Cake size:

Flavor: Shape:

Color scheme: Frosting:

Filling: Writing:

SPECIAL INSTRUCTIONS

PAYMENTS DETAILS

Total: Deposit: Total:

Cost: Paid: Paid:

Form of payment:

Order date:	Pickup ☐	**CAKE**
Delivery date:	Delivery ☐	**ORDER**
Order N:		**FORM**

CUSTOMER DETAILS

Name:

Address:

E-mail: Phone:

CAKE DETAILS

Cake type:	Tier:
Quantify:	Cake size:
Flavor:	Shape:
Color scheme:	Frosting:
Filling:	Writing:

SPECIAL INSTRUCTIONS

PAYMENTS DETAILS

Total:	Deposit:	Total:
Cost:	Paid:	Paid:
Form of payment:		

Order date:	Pickup ☐	## CAKE
Delivery date:	Delivery ☐	## ORDER
Order N:		## FORM

CUSTOMER DETAILS

Name:

Address:

E-mail: Phone:

CAKE DETAILS

Cake type:	Tier:
Quantify:	Cake size:
Flavor:	Shape:
Color scheme:	Frosting:
Filling:	Writing:

SPECIAL INSTRUCTIONS

PAYMENTS DETAILS

Total:	Deposit:	Total:
Cost:	Paid:	Paid:
Form of payment:		

Order date:⋯⋯⋯⋯ Pickup ☐

Delivery date:⋯⋯⋯⋯ Delivery ☐

Order N:⋯⋯⋯⋯

CAKE ORDER FORM

CUSTOMER DETAILS

Name:

Address:

E-mail: Phone:

CAKE DETAILS

Cake type: Tier:

Quantify: Cake size:

Flavor: Shape:

Color scheme: Frosting:

Filling: Writing:

SPECIAL INSTRUCTIONS

PAYMENTS DETAILS

Total: Deposit: Total:

Cost: Paid: Paid:

Form of payment:

Order date:	Pickup ☐	## CAKE ORDER FORM
Delivery date:	Delivery ☐	
Order N:		

CUSTOMER DETAILS

Name:

Address:

E-mail: Phone:

CAKE DETAILS

Cake type:	Tier:
Quantify:	Cake size:
Flavor:	Shape:
Color scheme:	Frosting:
Filling:	Writing:

SPECIAL INSTRUCTIONS

PAYMENTS DETAILS

Total:	Deposit:	Total:
Cost:	Paid:	Paid:
Form of payment:		

Order date: .... Pickup ☐

Delivery date: .... Delivery ☐

Order N: ....

CAKE ORDER FORM

CUSTOMER DETAILS

Name: ....

Address: ....

E-mail: .... Phone: ....

CAKE DETAILS

Cake type: .... Tier: ....

Quantify: .... Cake size: ....

Flavor: .... Shape: ....

Color scheme: .... Frosting: ....

Filling: .... Writing: ....

SPECIAL INSTRUCTIONS

PAYMENTS DETAILS

Total: .... Deposit: .... Total: ....

Cost: .... Paid: .... Paid: ....

Form of payment: ....

Order date:	Pickup ☐	**CAKE**
Delivery date:	Delivery ☐	**ORDER**
Order N:		**FORM**

CUSTOMER DETAILS

Name:

Address:

E-mail: Phone:

CAKE DETAILS

Cake type: Tier:

Quantify: Cake size:

Flavor: Shape:

Color scheme: Frosting:

Filling: Writing:

SPECIAL INSTRUCTIONS

PAYMENTS DETAILS

Total:	Deposit:	Total:
Cost:	Paid:	Paid:
Form of payment:		

Order date:	Pickup ☐	**CAKE**
Delivery date:	Delivery ☐	**ORDER**
Order N:		**FORM**

CUSTOMER DETAILS

Name:

Address:

E-mail: Phone:

CAKE DETAILS

Cake type: Tier:

Quantify: Cake size:

Flavor: Shape:

Color scheme: Frosting:

Filling: Writing:

SPECIAL INSTRUCTIONS

PAYMENTS DETAILS

Total: Deposit: Total:

Cost: Paid: Paid:

Form of payment:

Order date:	Pickup ☐	**CAKE ORDER FORM**
Delivery date:	Delivery ☐	
Order N:		

CUSTOMER DETAILS

Name:

Address:

E-mail: Phone:

CAKE DETAILS

Cake type:	Tier:
Quantify:	Cake size:
Flavor:	Shape:
Color scheme:	Frosting:
Filling:	Writing:

SPECIAL INSTRUCTIONS

PAYMENTS DETAILS

Total:	Deposit:	Total:
Cost:	Paid:	Paid:
Form of payment:		

Order date:	Pickup ☐	**CAKE**
Delivery date:	Delivery ☐	**ORDER**
Order N:		**FORM**

CUSTOMER DETAILS

Name:

Address:

E-mail: Phone:

CAKE DETAILS

Cake type:	Tier:
Quantify:	Cake size:
Flavor:	Shape:
Color scheme:	Frosting:
Filling:	Writing:

SPECIAL INSTRUCTIONS

PAYMENTS DETAILS

Total:	Deposit:	Total:
Cost:	Paid:	Paid:
Form of payment:		

Order date:	Pickup ☐
Delivery date:	Delivery ☐
Order N:	

CAKE ORDER FORM

CUSTOMER DETAILS

Name:

Address:

E-mail: Phone:

CAKE DETAILS

Cake type:	Tier:
Quantify:	Cake size:
Flavor:	Shape:
Color scheme:	Frosting:
Filling:	Writing:

SPECIAL INSTRUCTIONS

PAYMENTS DETAILS

Total:	Deposit:	Total:
Cost:	Paid:	Paid:
Form of payment:		

Order date: .... Pickup ☐

Delivery date: .... Delivery ☐

Order N: ....

CAKE ORDER FORM

CUSTOMER DETAILS

Name: ....

Address: ....

E-mail: .... Phone: ....

CAKE DETAILS

Cake type: .... Tier: ....

Quantify: .... Cake size: ....

Flavor: .... Shape: ....

Color scheme: .... Frosting: ....

Filling: .... Writing: ....

SPECIAL INSTRUCTIONS

PAYMENTS DETAILS

Total: .... Deposit: .... Total: ....

Cost: .... Paid: .... Paid: ....

Form of payment: ....

Order date:	Pickup ☐	# CAKE ORDER FORM
Delivery date:	Delivery ☐	
Order N:		

CUSTOMER DETAILS

Name:

Address:

E-mail: Phone:

CAKE DETAILS

Cake type: Tier:

Quantify: Cake size:

Flavor: Shape:

Color scheme: Frosting:

Filling: Writing:

SPECIAL INSTRUCTIONS

PAYMENTS DETAILS

Total: Deposit: Total:

Cost: Paid: Paid:

Form of payment:

Order date: .... Pickup ☐

Delivery date: .... Delivery ☐

Order N: ....

CAKE ORDER FORM

CUSTOMER DETAILS

Name: ....

Address: ....

E-mail: .... Phone: ....

CAKE DETAILS

Cake type: .... Tier: ....

Quantify: .... Cake size: ....

Flavor: .... Shape: ....

Color scheme: .... Frosting: ....

Filling: .... Writing: ....

SPECIAL INSTRUCTIONS

PAYMENTS DETAILS

Total: .... Deposit: .... Total: ....

Cost: .... Paid: .... Paid: ....

Form of payment: ....

Order date: .... Pickup ☐

Delivery date: .... Delivery ☐

Order N: ....

CAKE ORDER FORM

CUSTOMER DETAILS

Name:

Address:

E-mail: Phone:

CAKE DETAILS

Cake type: Tier:

Quantify: Cake size:

Flavor: Shape:

Color scheme: Frosting:

Filling: Writing:

SPECIAL INSTRUCTIONS

PAYMENTS DETAILS

Total: Deposit: Total:

Cost: Paid: Paid:

Form of payment:

Order date: .... Pickup ☐

Delivery date: .... Delivery ☐

Order N: ....

CAKE ORDER FORM

CUSTOMER DETAILS

Name:

Address:

E-mail: Phone:

CAKE DETAILS

Cake type: Tier:

Quantify: Cake size:

Flavor: Shape:

Color scheme: Frosting:

Filling: Writing:

SPECIAL INSTRUCTIONS

PAYMENTS DETAILS

Total: Deposit: Total:

Cost: Paid: Paid:

Form of payment:

Order date:................ Pickup ☐ Delivery date:................ Delivery ☐ Order N:................	**CAKE ORDER FORM**

CUSTOMER DETAILS

Name:

Address:

E-mail: Phone:

CAKE DETAILS

Cake type: Tier:

Quantify: Cake size:

Flavor: Shape:

Color scheme: Frosting:

Filling: Writing:

SPECIAL INSTRUCTIONS

PAYMENTS DETAILS

Total: Deposit: Total:

Cost: Paid: Paid:

Form of payment:

Order date:	Pickup ☐	**CAKE**
Delivery date:	Delivery ☐	**ORDER**
Order N:		**FORM**

CUSTOMER DETAILS

Name:

Address:

E-mail: Phone:

CAKE DETAILS

Cake type: Tier:

Quantify: Cake size:

Flavor: Shape:

Color scheme: Frosting:

Filling: Writing:

SPECIAL INSTRUCTIONS

PAYMENTS DETAILS

Total: Deposit: Total:

Cost: Paid: Paid:

Form of payment:

Order date:	Pickup ☐	**CAKE**
Delivery date:	Delivery ☐	**ORDER**
Order N:		**FORM**

CUSTOMER DETAILS

Name:

Address:

E-mail: Phone:

CAKE DETAILS

Cake type:	Tier:
Quantify:	Cake size:
Flavor:	Shape:
Color scheme:	Frosting:
Filling:	Writing:

SPECIAL INSTRUCTIONS

PAYMENTS DETAILS

Total:	Deposit:	Total:
Cost:	Paid:	Paid:
Form of payment:		

Order date: .... Pickup ☐

Delivery date: .... Delivery ☐

Order N: ....

CAKE ORDER FORM

CUSTOMER DETAILS

Name: ....

Address: ....

E-mail: .... Phone: ....

CAKE DETAILS

Cake type: .... Tier: ....

Quantify: .... Cake size: ....

Flavor: .... Shape: ....

Color scheme: .... Frosting: ....

Filling: .... Writing: ....

SPECIAL INSTRUCTIONS

....

....

....

....

PAYMENTS DETAILS

Total: .... Deposit: .... Total: ....

Cost: .... Paid: .... Paid: ....

Form of payment: ....

Order date:	Pickup ☐	### CAKE ORDER FORM
Delivery date:	Delivery ☐	
Order N:		

CUSTOMER DETAILS

Name:

Address:

E-mail: Phone:

CAKE DETAILS

Cake type: Tier:

Quantify: Cake size:

Flavor: Shape:

Color scheme: Frosting:

Filling: Writing:

SPECIAL INSTRUCTIONS

PAYMENTS DETAILS

Total: Deposit: Total:

Cost: Paid: Paid:

Form of payment:

	Order date:	Pickup ☐	# CAKE ORDER FORM
	Delivery date:	Delivery ☐	
	Order N:		

CUSTOMER DETAILS

Name:

Address:

E-mail: Phone:

CAKE DETAILS

Cake type:	Tier:
Quantify:	Cake size:
Flavor:	Shape:
Color scheme:	Frosting:
Filling:	Writing:

SPECIAL INSTRUCTIONS

PAYMENTS DETAILS

Total:	Deposit:	Total:
Cost:	Paid:	Paid:
Form of payment:		

Order date:	Pickup ☐	# CAKE
Delivery date:	Delivery ☐	# ORDER
Order N:		# FORM

CUSTOMER DETAILS

Name:

Address:

E-mail: Phone:

CAKE DETAILS

Cake type:	Tier:
Quantify:	Cake size:
Flavor:	Shape:
Color scheme:	Frosting:
Filling:	Writing:

SPECIAL INSTRUCTIONS

PAYMENTS DETAILS

Total:	Deposit:	Total:
Cost:	Paid:	Paid:
Form of payment:		

Order date: .... Pickup ☐

Delivery date: .... Delivery ☐

Order N: ....

CAKE ORDER FORM

CUSTOMER DETAILS

Name: ....

Address: ....

E-mail: .... Phone: ....

CAKE DETAILS

Cake type: .... Tier: ....

Quantify: .... Cake size: ....

Flavor: .... Shape: ....

Color scheme: .... Frosting: ....

Filling: .... Writing: ....

SPECIAL INSTRUCTIONS

....

....

....

....

PAYMENTS DETAILS

Total: .... Deposit: .... Total: ....

Cost: .... Paid: .... Paid: ....

Form of payment: ....

Order date:	Pickup ☐	## CAKE ORDER FORM
Delivery date:	Delivery ☐	
Order N:		

CUSTOMER DETAILS

Name:

Address:

E-mail: Phone:

CAKE DETAILS

Cake type:	Tier:
Quantify:	Cake size:
Flavor:	Shape:
Color scheme:	Frosting:
Filling:	Writing:

SPECIAL INSTRUCTIONS

PAYMENTS DETAILS

Total:	Deposit:	Total:
Cost:	Paid:	Paid:
Form of payment:		

Order date: .... Pickup ☐

Delivery date: .... Delivery ☐

Order N: ....

CAKE ORDER FORM

CUSTOMER DETAILS

Name: ....

Address: ....

E-mail: .... Phone: ....

CAKE DETAILS

Cake type: .... Tier: ....

Quantify: .... Cake size: ....

Flavor: .... Shape: ....

Color scheme: .... Frosting: ....

Filling: .... Writing: ....

SPECIAL INSTRUCTIONS

....

....

....

....

PAYMENTS DETAILS

Total: .... Deposit: .... Total: ....

Cost: .... Paid: .... Paid: ....

Form of payment: ....

Order date:	Pickup ☐	**CAKE ORDER FORM**
Delivery date:	Delivery ☐	
Order N:		

CUSTOMER DETAILS

Name:

Address:

E-mail: Phone:

CAKE DETAILS

Cake type:	Tier:
Quantify:	Cake size:
Flavor:	Shape:
Color scheme:	Frosting:
Filling:	Writing:

SPECIAL INSTRUCTIONS

PAYMENTS DETAILS

Total:	Deposit:	Total:
Cost:	Paid:	Paid:
Form of payment:		

Order date: .... Pickup ☐

Delivery date: .... Delivery ☐

Order N: ....

CAKE ORDER FORM

CUSTOMER DETAILS

Name: ....

Address: ....

E-mail: .... Phone: ....

CAKE DETAILS

Cake type: .... Tier: ....

Quantify: .... Cake size: ....

Flavor: .... Shape: ....

Color scheme: .... Frosting: ....

Filling: .... Writing: ....

SPECIAL INSTRUCTIONS

PAYMENTS DETAILS

Total: .... Deposit: .... Total: ....

Cost: .... Paid: .... Paid: ....

Form of payment: ....

Order date: .... Pickup ☐

Delivery date: .... Delivery ☐

Order N: ....

CAKE ORDER FORM

CUSTOMER DETAILS

Name:

Address:

E-mail: Phone:

CAKE DETAILS

Cake type: Tier:

Quantify: Cake size:

Flavor: Shape:

Color scheme: Frosting:

Filling: Writing:

SPECIAL INSTRUCTIONS

PAYMENTS DETAILS

Total: Deposit: Total:

Cost: Paid: Paid:

Form of payment:

Order date: .... Pickup ☐

Delivery date: .... Delivery ☐

Order N: ....

CAKE ORDER FORM

CUSTOMER DETAILS

Name:

Address:

E-mail: Phone:

CAKE DETAILS

Cake type:	Tier:
Quantify:	Cake size:
Flavor:	Shape:
Color scheme:	Frosting:
Filling:	Writing:

SPECIAL INSTRUCTIONS

PAYMENTS DETAILS

Total:	Deposit:	Total:
Cost:	Paid:	Paid:
Form of payment:		

Order date:	Pickup ☐	**CAKE**
Delivery date:	Delivery ☐	**ORDER**
Order N:		**FORM**

CUSTOMER DETAILS

Name:

Address:

E-mail: Phone:

CAKE DETAILS

Cake type:	Tier:
Quantify:	Cake size:
Flavor:	Shape:
Color scheme:	Frosting:
Filling:	Writing:

SPECIAL INSTRUCTIONS

PAYMENTS DETAILS

Total:	Deposit:	Total:
Cost:	Paid:	Paid:
Form of payment:		

Order date: .... Pickup ☐

Delivery date: .... Delivery ☐

Order N: ....

CAKE ORDER FORM

CUSTOMER DETAILS

Name:

Address:

E-mail: Phone:

CAKE DETAILS

Cake type: Tier:

Quantify: Cake size:

Flavor: Shape:

Color scheme: Frosting:

Filling: Writing:

SPECIAL INSTRUCTIONS

PAYMENTS DETAILS

Total: Deposit: Total:

Cost: Paid: Paid:

Form of payment:

Order date:................... Pickup ☐

Delivery date:................... Delivery ☐

Order N:...................

CAKE ORDER FORM

CUSTOMER DETAILS

Name:

Address:

E-mail: Phone:

CAKE DETAILS

Cake type: Tier:

Quantify: Cake size:

Flavor: Shape:

Color scheme: Frosting:

Filling: Writing:

SPECIAL INSTRUCTIONS

PAYMENTS DETAILS

Total: Deposit: Total:

Cost: Paid: Paid:

Form of payment:

Order date:	Pickup ☐	**CAKE**
Delivery date:	Delivery ☐	**ORDER**
Order N:		**FORM**

CUSTOMER DETAILS

Name:

Address:

E-mail: Phone:

CAKE DETAILS

Cake type: Tier:

Quantify: Cake size:

Flavor: Shape:

Color scheme: Frosting:

Filling: Writing:

SPECIAL INSTRUCTIONS

PAYMENTS DETAILS

Total: Deposit: Total:

Cost: Paid: Paid:

Form of payment:

Order date: .... Pickup ☐

Delivery date: .... Delivery ☐

Order N: ....

CAKE ORDER FORM

CUSTOMER DETAILS

Name: ....

Address: ....

E-mail: .... Phone: ....

CAKE DETAILS

Cake type: .... Tier: ....

Quantify: .... Cake size: ....

Flavor: .... Shape: ....

Color scheme: .... Frosting: ....

Filling: .... Writing: ....

SPECIAL INSTRUCTIONS

PAYMENTS DETAILS

Total: .... Deposit: .... Total: ....

Cost: .... Paid: .... Paid: ....

Form of payment: ....

	Order date:	Pickup ☐	**CAKE**
	Delivery date:	Delivery ☐	**ORDER**
	Order N:		**FORM**

CUSTOMER DETAILS

Name:	
Address:	
E-mail:	Phone:

CAKE DETAILS

Cake type:	Tier:
Quantify:	Cake size:
Flavor:	Shape:
Color scheme:	Frosting:
Filling:	Writing:

SPECIAL INSTRUCTIONS

PAYMENTS DETAILS

Total:	Deposit:	Total:
Cost:	Paid:	Paid:
Form of payment:		

Order date: .... Pickup ☐

Delivery date: .... Delivery ☐

Order N: ....

CAKE ORDER FORM

CUSTOMER DETAILS

Name: ....

Address: ....

E-mail: .... Phone: ....

CAKE DETAILS

Cake type: .... Tier: ....

Quantify: .... Cake size: ....

Flavor: .... Shape: ....

Color scheme: .... Frosting: ....

Filling: .... Writing: ....

SPECIAL INSTRUCTIONS

....

....

....

....

PAYMENTS DETAILS

Total: .... Deposit: .... Total: ....

Cost: .... Paid: .... Paid: ....

Form of payment: ....

Order date: _____ Pickup ☐

Delivery date: _____ Delivery ☐

Order N: _____

CAKE ORDER FORM

CUSTOMER DETAILS

Name:

Address:

E-mail: Phone:

CAKE DETAILS

Cake type: Tier:

Quantify: Cake size:

Flavor: Shape:

Color scheme: Frosting:

Filling: Writing:

SPECIAL INSTRUCTIONS

PAYMENTS DETAILS

Total: Deposit: Total:

Cost: Paid: Paid:

Form of payment:

Order date:	Pickup ☐	**CAKE**
Delivery date:	Delivery ☐	**ORDER**
Order N:		**FORM**

CUSTOMER DETAILS

Name:

Address:

E-mail: Phone:

CAKE DETAILS

Cake type:	Tier:
Quantify:	Cake size:
Flavor:	Shape:
Color scheme:	Frosting:
Filling:	Writing:

SPECIAL INSTRUCTIONS

PAYMENTS DETAILS

Total:	Deposit:	Total:
Cost:	Paid:	Paid:
Form of payment:		

Order date: .... Pickup ☐

Delivery date: .... Delivery ☐

Order N: ....

CAKE ORDER FORM

CUSTOMER DETAILS

Name:

Address:

E-mail: Phone:

CAKE DETAILS

Cake type: Tier:

Quantify: Cake size:

Flavor: Shape:

Color scheme: Frosting:

Filling: Writing:

SPECIAL INSTRUCTIONS

PAYMENTS DETAILS

Total: Deposit: Total:

Cost: Paid: Paid:

Form of payment:

Order date:	Pickup ☐	**CAKE ORDER FORM**
Delivery date:	Delivery ☐	
Order N:		

CUSTOMER DETAILS

Name:

Address:

E-mail: Phone:

CAKE DETAILS

Cake type:	Tier:
Quantify:	Cake size:
Flavor:	Shape:
Color scheme:	Frosting:
Filling:	Writing:

SPECIAL INSTRUCTIONS

PAYMENTS DETAILS

Total:	Deposit:	Total:
Cost:	Paid:	Paid:
Form of payment:		

Order date:	Pickup ☐	**CAKE**
Delivery date:	Delivery ☐	**ORDER**
Order N:		**FORM**

CUSTOMER DETAILS

Name:

Address:

E-mail: Phone:

CAKE DETAILS

Cake type:	Tier:
Quantify:	Cake size:
Flavor:	Shape:
Color scheme:	Frosting:
Filling:	Writing:

SPECIAL INSTRUCTIONS

PAYMENTS DETAILS

Total:	Deposit:	Total:
Cost:	Paid:	Paid:
Form of payment:		

Order date: ....   Pickup ☐

Delivery date: ....   Delivery ☐

Order N: ....

CAKE ORDER FORM

CUSTOMER DETAILS

Name:

Address:

E-mail: Phone:

CAKE DETAILS

Cake type: Tier:

Quantify: Cake size:

Flavor: Shape:

Color scheme: Frosting:

Filling: Writing:

SPECIAL INSTRUCTIONS

PAYMENTS DETAILS

Total: Deposit: Total:

Cost: Paid: Paid:

Form of payment:

Order date: .... Pickup ☐

Delivery date: .... Delivery ☐

Order N: ....

CAKE ORDER FORM

CUSTOMER DETAILS

Name: ....

Address: ....

E-mail: .... Phone: ....

CAKE DETAILS

Cake type: .... Tier: ....

Quantify: .... Cake size: ....

Flavor: .... Shape: ....

Color scheme: .... Frosting: ....

Filling: .... Writing: ....

SPECIAL INSTRUCTIONS

....

....

....

....

PAYMENTS DETAILS

Total: .... Deposit: .... Total: ....

Cost: .... Paid: .... Paid: ....

Form of payment: ....

Order date:................ Pickup ☐

Delivery date:................ Delivery ☐

Order N: ....

CAKE ORDER FORM

CUSTOMER DETAILS

Name:

Address:

E-mail: Phone:

CAKE DETAILS

Cake type: Tier:

Quantify: Cake size:

Flavor: Shape:

Color scheme: Frosting:

Filling: Writing:

SPECIAL INSTRUCTIONS

PAYMENTS DETAILS

Total: Deposit: Total:

Cost: Paid: Paid:

Form of payment:

Order date: .... Pickup ☐

Delivery date: .... Delivery ☐

Order N: ....

CAKE ORDER FORM

CUSTOMER DETAILS

Name: ....

Address: ....

E-mail: .... Phone: ....

CAKE DETAILS

Cake type: .... Tier: ....

Quantify: .... Cake size: ....

Flavor: .... Shape: ....

Color scheme: .... Frosting: ....

Filling: .... Writing: ....

SPECIAL INSTRUCTIONS

....

....

....

....

PAYMENTS DETAILS

Total: .... Deposit: .... Total: ....

Cost: .... Paid: .... Paid: ....

Form of payment: ....

Order date: .... Pickup ☐

Delivery date: .... Delivery ☐

Order N: ....

CAKE ORDER FORM

CUSTOMER DETAILS

Name:

Address:

E-mail: Phone:

CAKE DETAILS

Cake type: Tier:

Quantify: Cake size:

Flavor: Shape:

Color scheme: Frosting:

Filling: Writing:

SPECIAL INSTRUCTIONS

PAYMENTS DETAILS

Total: Deposit: Total:

Cost: Paid: Paid:

Form of payment:

Order date: .... Pickup ☐

Delivery date: .... Delivery ☐

Order N: ....

CAKE ORDER FORM

CUSTOMER DETAILS

Name: ....

Address: ....

E-mail: .... Phone: ....

CAKE DETAILS

Cake type: .... Tier: ....

Quantify: .... Cake size: ....

Flavor: .... Shape: ....

Color scheme: .... Frosting: ....

Filling: .... Writing: ....

SPECIAL INSTRUCTIONS

PAYMENTS DETAILS

Total: .... Deposit: .... Total: ....

Cost: .... Paid: .... Paid: ....

Form of payment: ....

Order date: .... Pickup ☐

Delivery date: .... Delivery ☐

Order N: ....

CAKE ORDER FORM

CUSTOMER DETAILS

Name:

Address:

E-mail: Phone:

CAKE DETAILS

Cake type: Tier:

Quantify: Cake size:

Flavor: Shape:

Color scheme: Frosting:

Filling: Writing:

SPECIAL INSTRUCTIONS

PAYMENTS DETAILS

Total: Deposit: Total:

Cost: Paid: Paid:

Form of payment:

Order date:	Pickup ☐	**CAKE**
Delivery date:	Delivery ☐	**ORDER**
Order N:		**FORM**

CUSTOMER DETAILS

Name:

Address:

E-mail: Phone:

CAKE DETAILS

Cake type:	Tier:
Quantify:	Cake size:
Flavor:	Shape:
Color scheme:	Frosting:
Filling:	Writing:

SPECIAL INSTRUCTIONS

PAYMENTS DETAILS

Total:	Deposit:	Total:
Cost:	Paid:	Paid:
Form of payment:		

CAKE ORDER FORM

Order date: .... Pickup ☐

Delivery date: .... Delivery ☐

Order N: ....

CUSTOMER DETAILS

Name:

Address:

E-mail: Phone:

CAKE DETAILS

Cake type: Tier:

Quantify: Cake size:

Flavor: Shape:

Color scheme: Frosting:

Filling: Writing:

SPECIAL INSTRUCTIONS

PAYMENTS DETAILS

Total: Deposit: Total:

Cost: Paid: Paid:

Form of payment:

Order date:................ Pickup ☐

Delivery date:................ Delivery ☐

Order N: ....

CAKE ORDER FORM

CUSTOMER DETAILS

Name:

Address:

E-mail: Phone:

CAKE DETAILS

Cake type: Tier:

Quantify: Cake size:

Flavor: Shape:

Color scheme: Frosting:

Filling: Writing:

SPECIAL INSTRUCTIONS

PAYMENTS DETAILS

Total: Deposit: Total:

Cost: Paid: Paid:

Form of payment:

Order date:	Pickup ☐	# CAKE ORDER FORM
Delivery date:	Delivery ☐	
Order N:		

CUSTOMER DETAILS

Name:

Address:

E-mail: Phone:

CAKE DETAILS

Cake type: Tier:

Quantify: Cake size:

Flavor: Shape:

Color scheme: Frosting:

Filling: Writing:

SPECIAL INSTRUCTIONS

PAYMENTS DETAILS

Total: Deposit: Total:

Cost: Paid: Paid:

Form of payment:

Order date:	Pickup ☐	**CAKE**
Delivery date:	Delivery ☐	**ORDER**
Order N:		**FORM**

CUSTOMER DETAILS

Name:

Address:

E-mail: Phone:

CAKE DETAILS

Cake type: Tier:

Quantify: Cake size:

Flavor: Shape:

Color scheme: Frosting:

Filling: Writing:

SPECIAL INSTRUCTIONS

PAYMENTS DETAILS

Total: Deposit: Total:

Cost: Paid: Paid:

Form of payment:

Order date:	Pickup ☐	**CAKE**
Delivery date:	Delivery ☐	**ORDER**
Order N:		**FORM**

CUSTOMER DETAILS

Name:

Address:

E-mail: Phone:

CAKE DETAILS

Cake type:	Tier:
Quantify:	Cake size:
Flavor:	Shape:
Color scheme:	Frosting:
Filling:	Writing:

SPECIAL INSTRUCTIONS

PAYMENTS DETAILS

Total:	Deposit:	Total:
Cost:	Paid:	Paid:
Form of payment:		

Order date: .... Pickup ☐

Delivery date: .... Delivery ☐

Order N: ....

CAKE ORDER FORM

CUSTOMER DETAILS

Name: ....

Address: ....

E-mail: .... Phone: ....

CAKE DETAILS

Cake type: .... Tier: ....

Quantify: .... Cake size: ....

Flavor: .... Shape: ....

Color scheme: .... Frosting: ....

Filling: .... Writing: ....

SPECIAL INSTRUCTIONS

....

....

....

....

PAYMENTS DETAILS

Total: .... Deposit: .... Total: ....

Cost: .... Paid: .... Paid: ....

Form of payment: ....

Order date: .... Pickup ☐

Delivery date: .... Delivery ☐

Order N: ....

CAKE ORDER FORM

CUSTOMER DETAILS

Name: ....

Address: ....

E-mail: .... Phone: ....

CAKE DETAILS

Cake type: .... Tier: ....

Quantify: .... Cake size: ....

Flavor: .... Shape: ....

Color scheme: .... Frosting: ....

Filling: .... Writing: ....

SPECIAL INSTRUCTIONS

....

....

....

....

PAYMENTS DETAILS

Total: .... Deposit: .... Total: ....

Cost: .... Paid: .... Paid: ....

Form of payment: ....

Order date: .... Pickup ☐

Delivery date: .... Delivery ☐

Order N: ....

CAKE ORDER FORM

CUSTOMER DETAILS

Name: ....

Address: ....

E-mail: .... Phone: ....

CAKE DETAILS

Cake type: .... Tier: ....

Quantify: .... Cake size: ....

Flavor: .... Shape: ....

Color scheme: .... Frosting: ....

Filling: .... Writing: ....

SPECIAL INSTRUCTIONS

....

....

....

....

PAYMENTS DETAILS

Total: .... Deposit: .... Total: ....

Cost: .... Paid: .... Paid: ....

Form of payment: ....

Order date:_____ Pickup ☐

Delivery date:_____ Delivery ☐

Order N:_____

CAKE ORDER FORM

CUSTOMER DETAILS

Name:

Address:

E-mail: Phone:

CAKE DETAILS

Cake type: Tier:

Quantify: Cake size:

Flavor: Shape:

Color scheme: Frosting:

Filling: Writing:

SPECIAL INSTRUCTIONS

PAYMENTS DETAILS

Total: Deposit: Total:

Cost: Paid: Paid:

Form of payment:

Order date:	Pickup ☐	# CAKE
Delivery date:	Delivery ☐	# ORDER
Order N:		# FORM

CUSTOMER DETAILS

Name:

Address:

E-mail: Phone:

CAKE DETAILS

Cake type: Tier:

Quantify: Cake size:

Flavor: Shape:

Color scheme: Frosting:

Filling: Writing:

SPECIAL INSTRUCTIONS

PAYMENTS DETAILS

Total: Deposit: Total:

Cost: Paid: Paid:

Form of payment:

	CAKE ORDER FORM
Order date: .... Pickup ☐	
Delivery date: .... Delivery ☐	
Order N:	

CUSTOMER DETAILS

Name:

Address:

E-mail: Phone:

CAKE DETAILS

Cake type:	Tier:
Quantify:	Cake size:
Flavor:	Shape:
Color scheme:	Frosting:
Filling:	Writing:

SPECIAL INSTRUCTIONS

PAYMENTS DETAILS

Total:	Deposit:	Total:
Cost:	Paid:	Paid:
Form of payment:		

Order date: .... Pickup ☐

Delivery date: .... Delivery ☐

Order N: ....

CAKE ORDER FORM

CUSTOMER DETAILS

Name: ....

Address: ....

E-mail: .... Phone: ....

CAKE DETAILS

Cake type: .... Tier: ....

Quantify: .... Cake size: ....

Flavor: .... Shape: ....

Color scheme: .... Frosting: ....

Filling: .... Writing: ....

SPECIAL INSTRUCTIONS

....

....

....

....

PAYMENTS DETAILS

Total: .... Deposit: .... Total: ....

Cost: .... Paid: .... Paid: ....

Form of payment: ....

Order date: .... Pickup ☐

Delivery date: .... Delivery ☐

Order N: ....

CAKE ORDER FORM

CUSTOMER DETAILS

Name:

Address:

E-mail: Phone:

CAKE DETAILS

Cake type: Tier:

Quantify: Cake size:

Flavor: Shape:

Color scheme: Frosting:

Filling: Writing:

SPECIAL INSTRUCTIONS

PAYMENTS DETAILS

Total: Deposit: Total:

Cost: Paid: Paid:

Form of payment:

Order date: .... Pickup ☐

Delivery date: .... Delivery ☐

Order N: ....

CAKE ORDER FORM

CUSTOMER DETAILS

Name: ....

Address: ....

E-mail: .... Phone: ....

CAKE DETAILS

Cake type: .... Tier: ....

Quantify: .... Cake size: ....

Flavor: .... Shape: ....

Color scheme: .... Frosting: ....

Filling: .... Writing: ....

SPECIAL INSTRUCTIONS

....

....

....

....

PAYMENTS DETAILS

Total: .... Deposit: .... Total: ....

Cost: .... Paid: .... Paid: ....

Form of payment: ....

Order date: .... Pickup ☐

Delivery date: .... Delivery ☐

Order N: ....

CAKE ORDER FORM

CUSTOMER DETAILS

Name:

Address:

E-mail: Phone:

CAKE DETAILS

Cake type:	Tier:
Quantify:	Cake size:
Flavor:	Shape:
Color scheme:	Frosting:
Filling:	Writing:

SPECIAL INSTRUCTIONS

PAYMENTS DETAILS

Total:	Deposit:	Total:
Cost:	Paid:	Paid:
Form of payment:		

Order date:	Pickup ☐
Delivery date:	Delivery ☐
Order N:	

CAKE ORDER FORM

CUSTOMER DETAILS

Name:

Address:

E-mail: Phone:

CAKE DETAILS

Cake type:	Tier:
Quantify:	Cake size:
Flavor:	Shape:
Color scheme:	Frosting:
Filling:	Writing:

SPECIAL INSTRUCTIONS

PAYMENTS DETAILS

Total:	Deposit:	Total:
Cost:	Paid:	Paid:
Form of payment:		

Order date:	Pickup ☐	CAKE
Delivery date:	Delivery ☐	ORDER
Order N:		FORM

CUSTOMER DETAILS

Name:

Address:

E-mail: Phone:

CAKE DETAILS

Cake type: Tier:

Quantify: Cake size:

Flavor: Shape:

Color scheme: Frosting:

Filling: Writing:

SPECIAL INSTRUCTIONS

PAYMENTS DETAILS

Total: Deposit: Total:

Cost: Paid: Paid:

Form of payment:

Order date:	Pickup ☐	## CAKE ORDER FORM
Delivery date:	Delivery ☐	
Order N:		

CUSTOMER DETAILS

Name:

Address:

E-mail: Phone:

CAKE DETAILS

Cake type:	Tier:
Quantify:	Cake size:
Flavor:	Shape:
Color scheme:	Frosting:
Filling:	Writing:

SPECIAL INSTRUCTIONS

PAYMENTS DETAILS

Total:	Deposit:	Total:
Cost:	Paid:	Paid:
Form of payment:		

Order date:_____ Pickup ☐

Delivery date:_____ Delivery ☐

Order N:_____

CAKE ORDER FORM

CUSTOMER DETAILS

Name:

Address:

E-mail: Phone:

CAKE DETAILS

Cake type: Tier:

Quantify: Cake size:

Flavor: Shape:

Color scheme: Frosting:

Filling: Writing:

SPECIAL INSTRUCTIONS

PAYMENTS DETAILS

Total: Deposit: Total:

Cost: Paid: Paid:

Form of payment:

Order date: .... Pickup ☐

Delivery date: .... Delivery ☐

Order N: ....

CAKE ORDER FORM

CUSTOMER DETAILS

Name: ....

Address: ....

E-mail: .... Phone: ....

CAKE DETAILS

Cake type: .... Tier: ....

Quantify: .... Cake size: ....

Flavor: .... Shape: ....

Color scheme: .... Frosting: ....

Filling: .... Writing: ....

SPECIAL INSTRUCTIONS

....

....

....

....

PAYMENTS DETAILS

Total: .... Deposit: .... Total: ....

Cost: .... Paid: .... Paid: ....

Form of payment: ....

Order date: .... Pickup ☐

Delivery date: .... Delivery ☐

Order N: ....

CAKE ORDER FORM

CUSTOMER DETAILS

Name:

Address:

E-mail: Phone:

CAKE DETAILS

Cake type: Tier:

Quantify: Cake size:

Flavor: Shape:

Color scheme: Frosting:

Filling: Writing:

SPECIAL INSTRUCTIONS

PAYMENTS DETAILS

Total: Deposit: Total:

Cost: Paid: Paid:

Form of payment:

Order date:	Pickup ☐	**CAKE ORDER FORM**
Delivery date:	Delivery ☐	
Order N:		

CUSTOMER DETAILS

Name:

Address:

E-mail: Phone:

CAKE DETAILS

Cake type:	Tier:
Quantify:	Cake size:
Flavor:	Shape:
Color scheme:	Frosting:
Filling:	Writing:

SPECIAL INSTRUCTIONS

PAYMENTS DETAILS

Total:	Deposit:	Total:
Cost:	Paid:	Paid:
Form of payment:		